Highlights

BEST

HIDDEN PICTURES PUZZLES

EVER

HIGHLIGHTS PRESS
Honesdale, Pennsylvania

W9-AKT-740

75 Years of Hidden Pictures

In June 1946, Garry Cleveland Myers and Caroline Clark Myers published the first issue of *Highlights for Children*, a monthly magazine full of stories, puzzles, and creative thinking. Did you know that there was a Hidden Pictures puzzle in the very first issue? You can solve it on the next page! Although, disembodied limbs wouldn't be hidden objects in puzzles created today.

Hidden Pictures puzzles quickly became the most popular feature in the magazine. And, as Highlights grew, so did the types of puzzles. Over 75 years, Hidden Pictures puzzles have evolved from black and white into color and beyond. There is a wide variety of art styles—including photographic puzzles, digital puzzles, and even puzzles with hidden words instead of objects.

In this book, you can put your sleuthing skills to the test and try out many of these different puzzle types. But don't worry— there are answers at the back of the book, so no banana will remain unfound.

Happy puzzling!

This is the very first Hidden Pictures puzzle from the June 1946 issue of *Highlights* magazine.

HIGHLIGHTS
FOR CHILDREN

fun WITH A PURPOSE

The cost of a one-year *Highlights* subscription in 1946 was $4.00.

Find the alarm clock, arm and hand, bird, child's face, dog's head, fairy princess, fish, hammer, shoe, turtle, umbrella, and woman's face.

I'm snailing this delivery!

Can you find 18 envelopes hiding in the scene above?

The **75th** birthday issue in June 2021 was the **836th**. Each one has had a Hidden Pictures puzzle in it!

In **75** years, more than **135,000** objects have been hidden in more than **9,800** puzzles.

The first issue of *Highlights* in June 1946 reached about 20,000 American children. Today, Highlights magazines reach more than **2 million** kids each month.

The **billionth** copy of *Highlights* was printed in **2006**. One billion copies of *Highlights* magazine side by side would wrap around the earth **FIVE** times!

Mixed-Up Covers

We've mixed up eight *Highlights* covers from the past seven decades.
See if you can match the cover with the year it was published.

| 1946 | 1956 | 1966 | 1976 |
| 1986 | 1996 | 2006 | 2011 |

Since **1955**, many children have first discovered *Highlights* in a doctor's or dentist's waiting room.

flashlight

suitcase

pen

party horn

plunger

necktie

golf club

banana

lotion bottle

蜡烛　　　女子　　　手套　　　梳子　　　针　　　书

牙刷　　　胡萝卜　　　回形针　　　铅笔　　　香蕉　　　心　　　鱼　　　一块馅饼

sock

ruler

comb

scarf

heart

pen

mitten

pitcher

boot

vase

kite

sailboat

I Found It!

**What's your favorite way to solve a Hidden Pictures puzzle?
There are TONS of different ways, including:**

- Circling the object
- Drawing an X on the object
- Making a check mark
- Coloring in the object

with a

- pencil
- pen
- marker
- crayon

on the

- clue box
- big picture

From A to Z, here are the most unusual objects ever hidden.

Rafting is bear-y fun!

accordion

bear in a raft

cement block

dancing flute

éclair

fish skeleton

game controller

This is hidden in a puzzle in this book. Can you find it?

hobby horse

island

Know any good pitcher jokes?

jukebox

kazoo

Over the years, we've hidden **7** kazoos, **5** banjos, and **2** ukuleles.

laughing pitcher

metronome

North Pole

overalls

The check? Just put it on my bill.

platypus

quill and ink

radiator

This is hidden in a puzzle in this book. Can you find it?

scuba tank

tic-tac-toe game

utensils

vacuum

walrus

X-ray

yogurt cup

This is hidden in a puzzle in this book. Can you find it?

zeppelin

The game controller is on page 115, the scuba tank is on page 69, and the yogurt cup is on page 59.

TOP 10 HIDDEN OBJECTS

What are the top 10 most frequently hidden objects?
Find all 10 in this puzzle, then find out where they rank on the following pages.

#10 NEEDLES

Can you find 12 hidden needles?

#9 SAILBOATS

Can you find 12 hidden sailboats?

Blades

Frond

Bladder

Stipe

Holdfast

#8 SPOONS

Can you find 12 hidden spoons?

Can you find 12 hidden candles?

#6 CRESCENT MOONS

Can you find 12 hidden crescent moons?

Can you find 12 hidden hearts?

missing 1

#4 FISH

Can you find 12 hidden fish?

AaaAaA'.

#3 TOOTHBRUSHES

Can you find 12 hidden toothbrushes?

#2 BANANAS

Can you find 12 hidden bananas?

Can you find 12 hidden pencils?

Hide It!

Now that you've found 12 ways to hide pencils, can you hide this pencil in your own Hidden Pictures drawing?

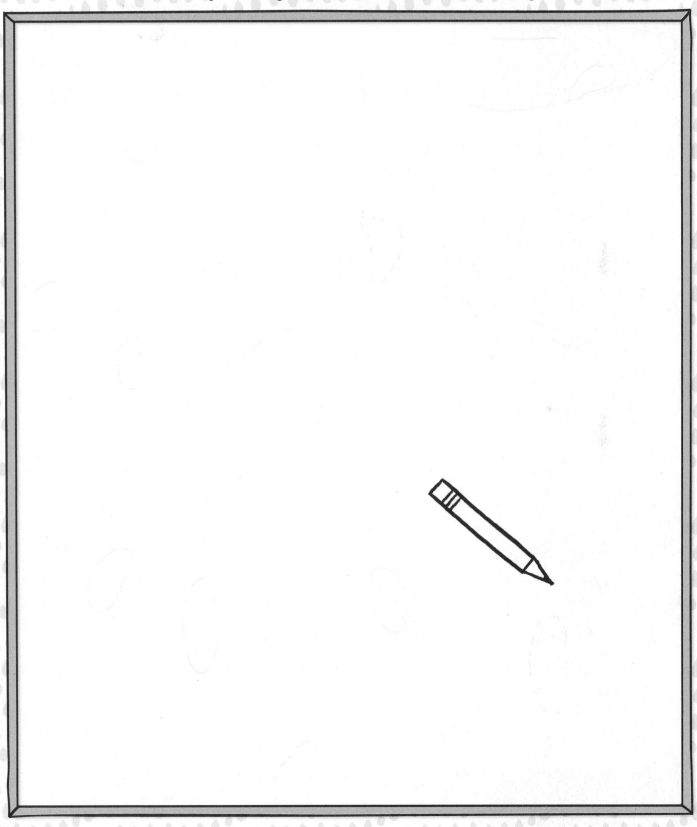

whale

toothbrush

envelope

paper clip

pencil

sailboat

ruler

light bulb

fishhook

canoe

heart

sock

banana

mug

bell

Still sharpening your pencils? There are **31** hidden pencils in this book. Start by finding one of them at this hoedown—along with the **14** other objects.

BONUS!
Can you find the crayon, teacup, golf club, and feather?

snake

screwdriver

traffic cone

musical note

open book

hot dog

banana

ice pop

hairbrush

heart

diamond ring

carrot

question mark

artist's brush

baseball cap

Each of these scenes contains **12** hidden objects, which are listed on the next page. But each object is only **hidden once**. Which object is in which scene?

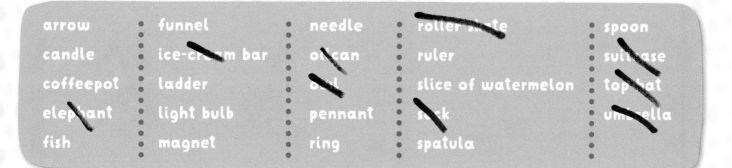

arrow	funnel	needle	roller skate	spoon
candle	ice-cream bar	oil can	ruler	suitcase
coffeepot	ladder	owl	slice of watermelon	top hat
elephant	light bulb	pennant	sock	umbrella
fish	magnet	ring	spatula	

Horseshoe shopping is fun!

sailboat

balloon

slice of pizza

party hat

envelope

mushroom

feather

flower

ruler

banana

bowling pin

crown

fork · heart · cotton candy · bell · candy cane · sock · slice of pie · teacup · boomerang · horseshoe · toothbrush · golf club · pencil · ring · fish · crown · fishhook

HONESDALE ZOO BASEBALL STARS

The Highlights editorial offices are in Honesdale, Pennsylvania. There isn't a zoo there, though!

golf club

envelope

spider

crescent moon

spoon

worm

ring

bell

house

toothbrush

banana

mug

button

sailboat

Your downward dog pose is improving!

Can you find 5 hidden objects that can all be found at a baseball game?

baseball

baseball cap

baseball glove

baseball diamond

baseball bat

Zatz and Zurkle

Here's what Zatz and Zurkle called the objects they found. Can you find them, too?

flingala

sritchit

koobah

upzee

glork

kupple

snoofle

fried immy

cribble

pipo

krustoa

floosh

tiggly

cubeedoo

Can you believe they go on another ride after this? It tumbles them around until they are warm and toasty. Plus, they get to come back every week!

I'm a little jealous, Zatz. And a little dizzy.

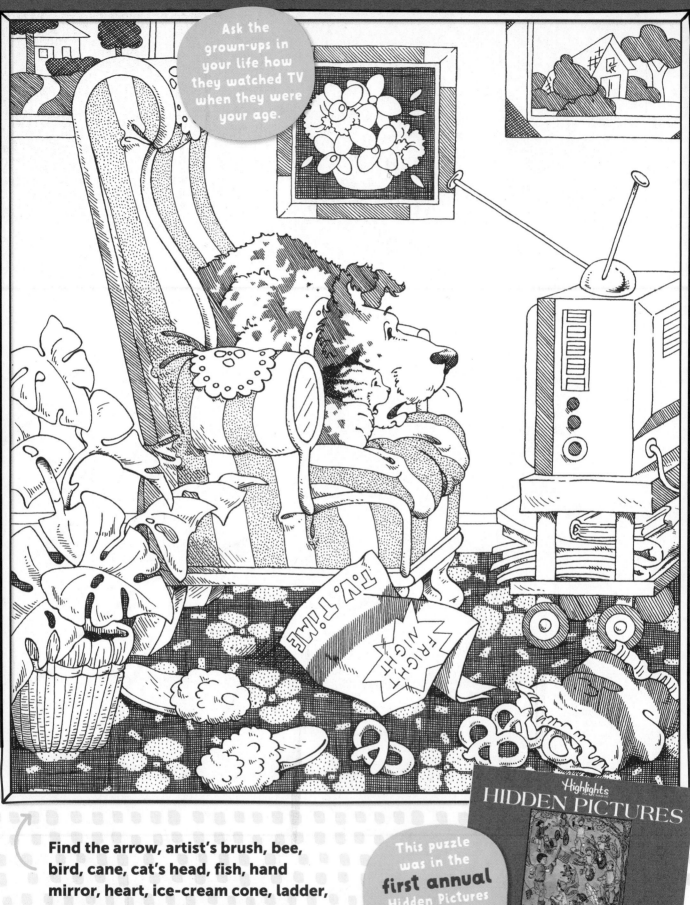

Ask the grown-ups in your life how they watched TV when they were your age.

Find the arrow, artist's brush, bee, bird, cane, cat's head, fish, hand mirror, heart, ice-cream cone, ladder, letter *F*, letter *L*, letter *U*, letter *V*, pennant, sheep, and trowel.

This puzzle was in the **first annual** Hidden Pictures Calendar in **1994**

Were these paintings done by copycats?

leaf
wedge of lemon
light bulb
toothbrush
fried egg
heart
umbrella
rainbow
necktie
ice-cream cone
fork
apple
ring
high-heeled shoe
carrot
crown
slice of watermelon

flag

golf club

crescent moon

toothbrush

musical note

ring

teacup

envelope

shoe

candle

baseball hat

comb

spatula

crayon

ice-cream cone

candy corn

fish

40

Double Cross

To find the answer to the riddle below, first cross out all the pairs of matching letters. Then write the remaining letters in order in the spaces at the bottom of the page. Then find the 5 hidden objects.

PP	AA	NO	LL	QQ	NE
LL	TH	OO	ZZ	EY	SS
HA	FF	DD	VE	CC	MM
JJ	YY	BE	GG	EE	AR
RR	FE	II	KK	BB	NN
XX	HH	TT	UU	ET	VV

What type of socks do polar bears wear?

_____ . ___ ____

There are **16** socks hidden in this puzzle. Can you find them all?

Say each one three times fast!

SANDY'S SHELL SOCKS SHRUNK.

OKSANA WASHED SOME AWESOME SOCKS.

MITCH MATCHED MISSY'S MISMATCHED SOCKS.

Hide It!

Now that you've found 16 ways to hide socks, can you hide this sock in your own Hidden Pictures drawing?

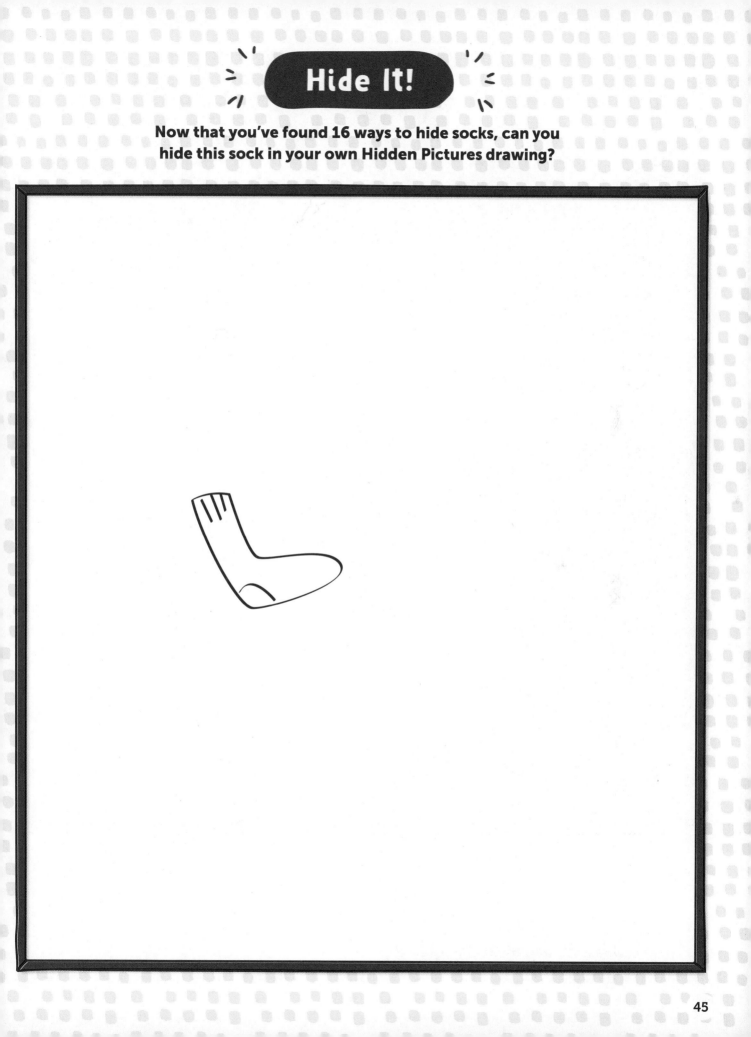

drumstick

golf tee

envelope

spool of thread

kite

teacup

fish

sock

towel

arrowhead

mushroom

necktie

ice-cream cone

boomerang

tack

butterfly

shoe

lightning bolt

sailboat

needle

clover

pennant

canoe

snake

bell

Why did the ice-cream cone read the newspaper?
. . . .
To get the latest scoop

Why did the math teacher read the newspaper?
. . . .
To check the ad section

Why did the werewolf read the newspaper?
. . . .
To check his horror-scope

Why did the electric eel read the newspaper?
. . . .
To keep up on current events

Ha Ha HA HA HA Ha Ha

We're going to need something to clean up this mess . . .

toothbrush

banana

adhesive bandage

belt

sailboat

button

glue

ring

rake

envelope

wristwatch

oven mitt

tack

slice of pizza

artist's brush

There's a sponge hidden somewhere around here!

ice-cream cone
button
ruler
ladder
envelope
pennant
sponge
nail
golf club
slice of pie
comb
teacup
ladle

What are these dogs dreaming about?
Imagine and draw it, then try to find 5 hidden objects.

In case the dogs are dreaming about bones, there's a hidden bone over here!

cup
fish
bell
crayon
dog bone
arrow
heart
pointy hat
magic lamp
whale
goose
seashell
mallet
yam
slice of pie
pennant
hockey stick
spatula
drinking straw

51

6 by Six

Each of these small scenes contains 6 hidden objects from the list below. Some objects are hidden in more than one scene. Can you find the 6 hidden objects in each scene?

comb (3)	pitcher (3)
drumstick (4)	slice of pizza (2)
flashlight (3)	teacup (3)
lollipop (2)	toothbrush (3)
mitten (3)	waffle (2)
nail (3)	yo-yo (5)

The numbers tell you how many times each object is hidden.

BONUS MATCH

Two scenes contain the exact same set of hidden objects. Can you find that matching pair?

A Silly Fill-In Story

Uh-oh! Hidden objects have taken over this story. Each teal word below is also a hidden object in the big picture on the next page. Can you find them all?

My birthday is my favorite **BAGEL** of the year. So it was even more awesome that, this year, my friends all threw me a surprise **ENVELOPE** in the backyard! What could be better? Oscar and Bella made my favorite foods, like **LAMPSHADE** muffins, pepperoni-and-**TOOTHBRUSH** pizza, and a big **LOCK** of ice-cold **CRESCENT MOON**. Rosie and Buddy set up my favorite games to play: Pin the **MALLET** on the **ICE-CREAM CONE** and Duck, Duck, **PAPER CLIP**. Just when I thought this birthday couldn't be any more perfect, Daisy brought out the special **RING** that she had baked and frosted with my favorite color of icing—**ICE SKATE**. And, of course, the dessert was my very favorite kind: a three-layer **SOCK** cake! All my friends sang, and then I blew out each and every **SLIPPER**. And my friend Clark gave me a super gift—a brand-new **SLICE OF PIZZA**. How did he know it was just what I wished for? It was an awesome bark-day!

Find the candle, canoe, fish, king, pumpkin, queen, skate, slipper, and whale.

Highlights for Children
NOVEMBER 1997

Fun with a Purpose®

This library scene is from the **November 1997** issue of Highlights.

Find the banana, crayon, hammer, mushroom, paintbrush, shoe, shovel, slice of cake, slice of pie, spatula, spoon, and toothbrush.

Not all Hidden Pictures puzzles have hidden objects. This one has **WORDS**. Can you find PINK, DANCE, TWIRL, BEACH, SAND, SUN, BIRD, and TUTU?

Tongue Twisters

Say each one three times fast!

TOOTIE TORE HER TURQUOISE TUTU.

FIVE FUN-LOVING FLAMINGOS FROLIC.

TRAVIS TELLS TERRI TO TWIRL.

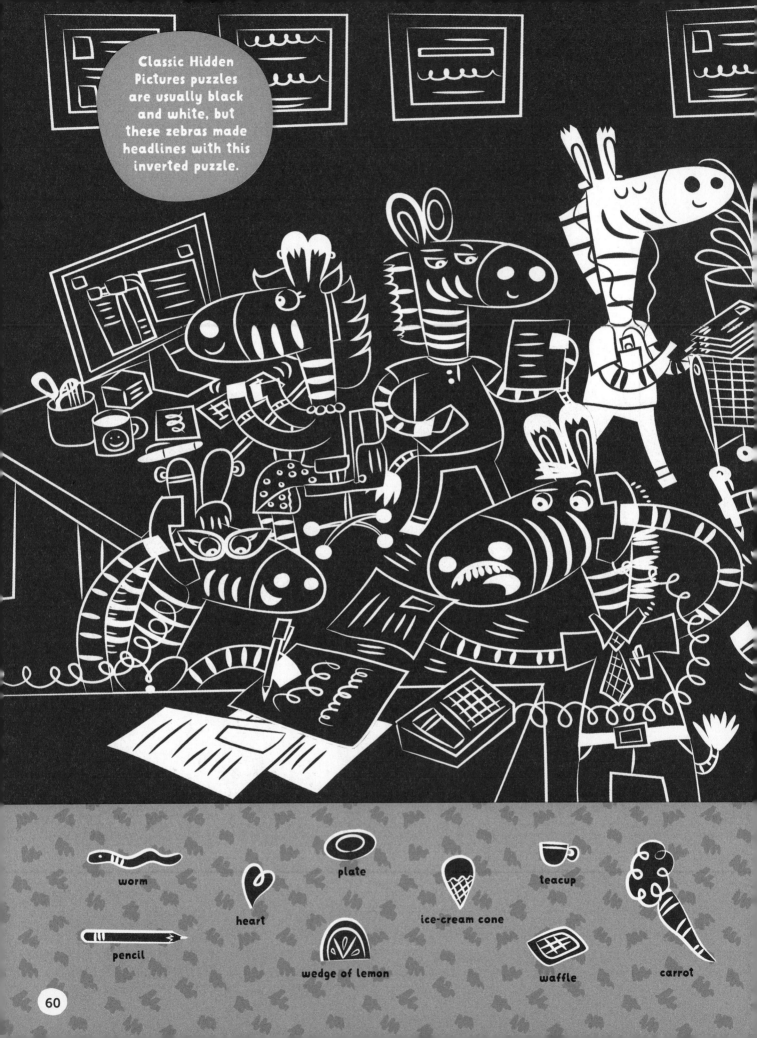

Classic Hidden Pictures puzzles are usually black and white, but these zebras made headlines with this inverted puzzle.

worm

plate

teacup

heart

ice-cream cone

pencil

wedge of lemon

waffle

carrot

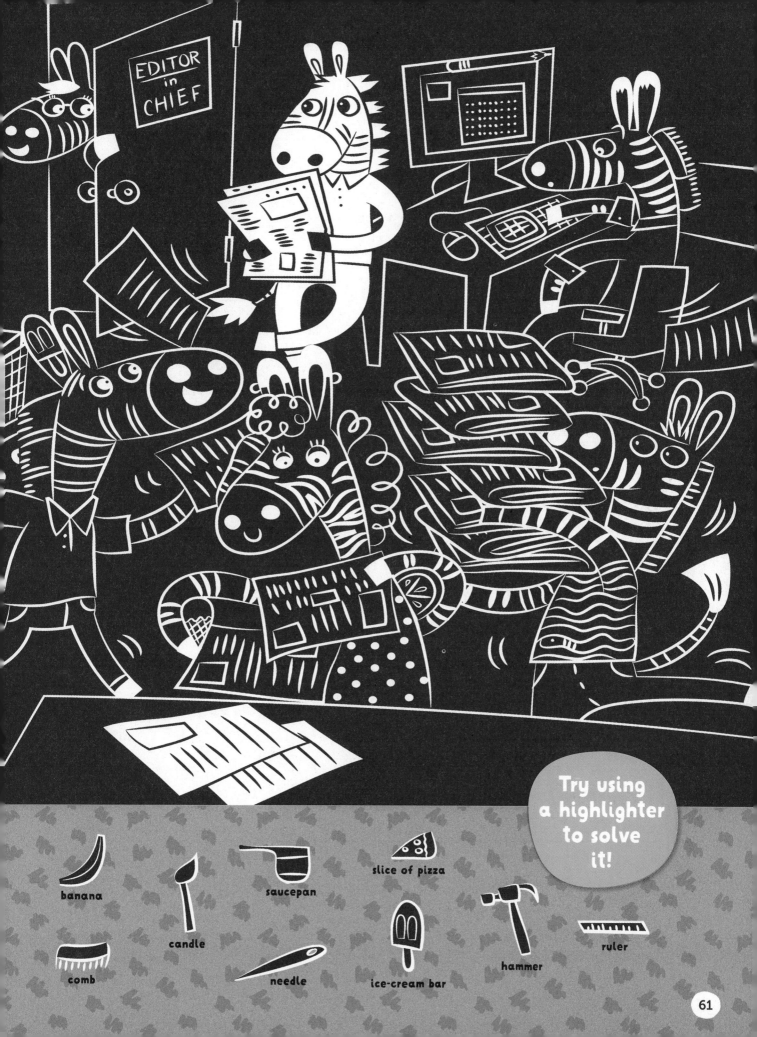

EDITOR in CHIEF

Try using a highlighter to solve it!

banana

candle

comb

saucepan

needle

slice of pizza

ice-cream bar

hammer

ruler

Hidden Word Search

Why are pine trees such bad knitters?

They are always dropping their needles.

You can find everything you need for a new knitting project at Nicole's. Can you find the 15 hidden objects?

pizza
hair dryer
fish
domino
party hat
iron
wedge of lime
beehive
egg
horseshoe
hanger
briefcase
sailboat
seashell
drinking straw

The **hidden objects** are
hidden words, too. Can you find
them in the letters below? We found
the first one for you.

h	w	t	x	m	i	v	d	a	s
s	e	a	s	h	e	l	l	r	u
h	d	o	m	i	n	o	i	e	i
o	g	b	d	c	t	r	t	g	t
r	e	l	i	a	o	q	a	n	c
s	o	i	a	n	x	e	h	a	a
e	f	a	u	e	v	a	y	h	s
s	l	s	n	i	m	a	t	t	e
h	i	r	h	y	z	p	r	a	c
o	o	m	e	s	z	h	s	a	o	f
e	e	u	i	t	c	h	p	c	b
b	v	p	f	i	y	j	e	g	n
e	n	v	c	j	f	p	m	g	e
r	h	a	i	r	d	r	y	e	r

The artist who drew this scene holds the record for creating the most Hidden Pictures puzzles—**549**!

More than **500** illustrators have created more than **9,800** Hidden Pictures puzzles.

fish
glove
can
butterfly
star
ice-cream cone
mug
high-heeled shoe
mushroom
saw
pennant
paper clip
nail
mitten
golf club
banana
balloon

66

This puzzle is just one-twelfth of *The Longest Hidden Pictures Puzzle Ever.* At **16** feet, **9** inches, it's a **Guinness World Record** holder!

sailboat

elephant

candy cane

seashell

fish

game piece

light bulb

wrench

croissant

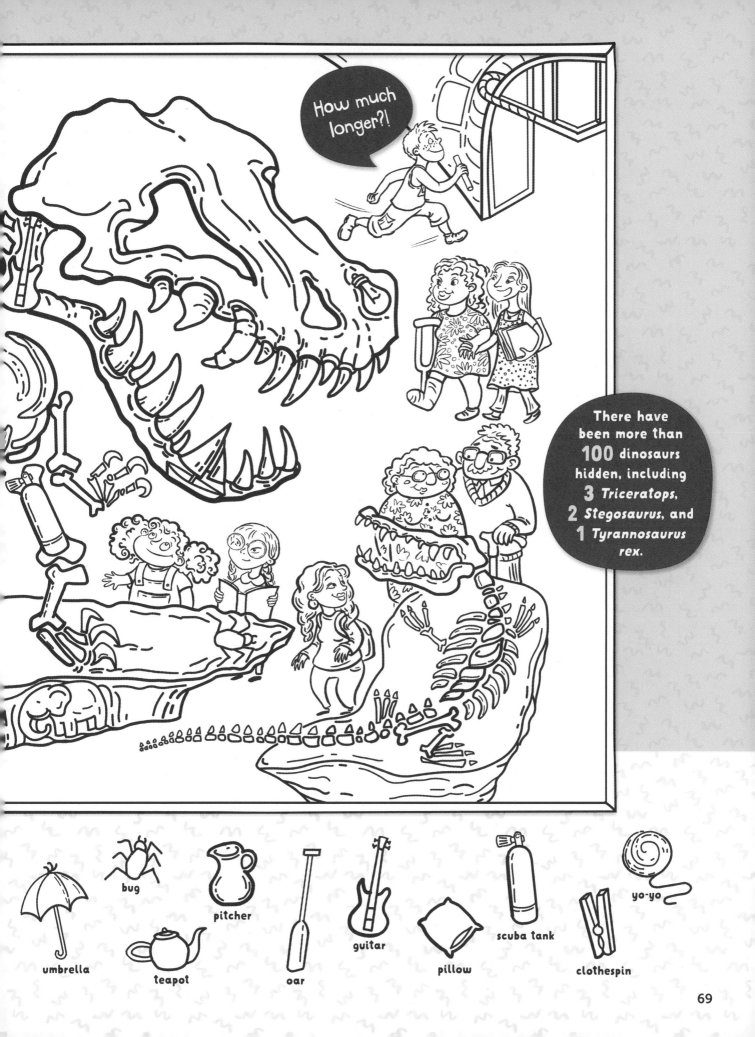

Words and Objects

There are **8 OBJECTS** hidden on this page that match the **8 WORDS** hidden on the next page. Can you find them all?

comb
crescent moon
mitten
paintbrush
paper clip
pencil
sock
teacup

This rock band hits all the right notes!

flower wheel mug book envelope spoon carrot crescent moon basketball shoe

fish toothbrush key slice of pizza ice-cream cone pencil banana hammer

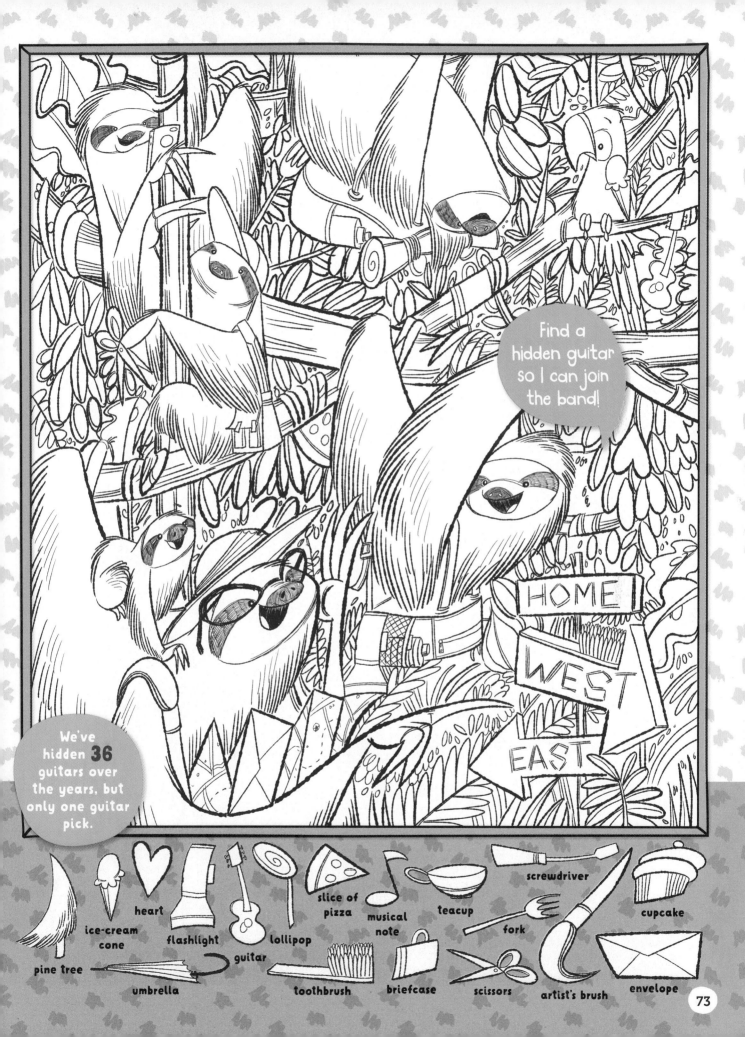

Find a hidden guitar so I can join the band!

We've hidden **36** guitars over the years, but only one guitar pick.

HOME
WEST
EAST

pine tree

ice-cream cone

heart

flashlight

guitar

umbrella

lollipop

slice of pizza

musical note

toothbrush

briefcase

teacup

scissors

fork

screwdriver

artist's brush

cupcake

envelope

Find the anchor, ant, bird, cup and saucer, fish, pig, rabbit's head, shoe, sickle, teddy bear, toad, treble clef, and wishbone.

First appearing in the **May 1954** issue of *Highlights*, this puzzle was inspired by the fairy tale "The Princess and the Pea."

This similarly inspired scene is from the **2005 Hidden Pictures** book.

Find the baseball bat, bottle, dog bone, fish, mitten, mug, mushroom, open book, paintbrush, saltshaker, slice of cake, slice of pie, spool of thread, and toothbrush.

Put on your goggles to solve this puzzle, then find the **39** hidden fish throughout the book.

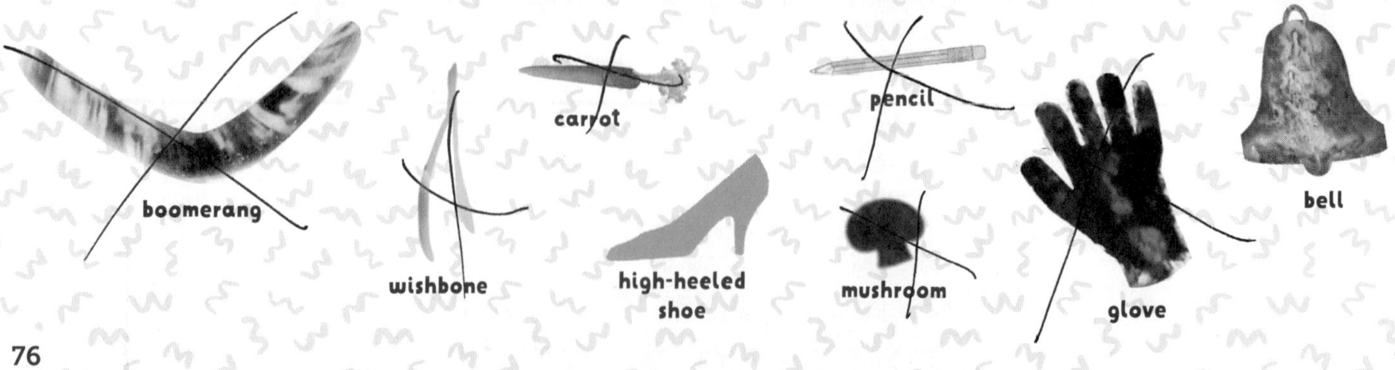

boomerang

carrot

pencil

bell

wishbone

high-heeled shoe

mushroom

glove

apple

cupcake

slice of
pizza

canoe

light bulb

hourglass

dog bone

sailboat

ax

banana   ladder   slice of bread   pencil   spatula   envelope   toothbrush   spoon   teacup   fried egg   sock   kite   domino   heart   bell   magnifying glass   cookie

Find this suitcase and the **23** other objects below.

crescent moon

toothbrush

candy corn

golf club

pencil

slice of pie

sailboat

pen

crayon

boomerang

banana

drinking straw

candle

feather

sock

slice of bread

glove

muffin

acorn

artist's brush

toothbrush

nail

hockey stick

FRESH FISH

Would you be more surprised to see polar bears at a grocery store . . .

key
hockey stick
hat
banana
pennant
crayon
comb
bell
hairbrush
yo-yo
crown
tack
crescent moon
slice of pie
heart
shovel
graham cracker
candle
sock
horn
ruler

80

... or to see a toucan driving a tractor?

wedge of lemon

trowel

walnut

slice of bread

baseball bat

arrow

hanger

pennant

horn

candle

umbrella

elf's hat

doughnut

fishhook

snowman

paper clip

bean

shoe

marshmallow

bell

screwdriver

adhesive bandage

cupcake

artist's brush

mushroom

knitted hat

lightning bolt

apple

tweezers

strawberry

boomerang

pear

top hat

spoon

candle

lamp

tack

screw

golf tee

toothbrush

mitten

sailboat

butter knife

checker

ice pop

egg

wedge of lemon

ax

magnet

thimble

magnifying glass

lemon

fan

candy cane

crown

bean

bowl

needle

teacup

crescent moon

book

porcupine

high-heeled shoe

cotton candy

flag

butterfly

heart

ring

olive

Hide It!

Pick one of the objects above and hide it in your own Hidden Pictures drawing.

Out of Charm's Way

Kevin had his 10th birthday party at the new rock-climbing wall in the park. He invited all his friends—including Heidi and Zeke. Everyone had a blast climbing. But when it was time to go home, Kevin's friend Nora burst into tears. Her charm bracelet was missing!

"I took it off before climbing and put it in the grass near the wall," said Nora. "Now it's gone."

Heidi and Zeke ran over to help. Zeke checked the grass while Heidi searched the picnic area. When she was done, she looked over and saw Zeke standing up with his front paws on the wall.

"Zeke! Dogs can't climb!" shouted Heidi. Then something caught her eye. "But maybe bracelets can!"

Look for the missing bracelet.
Then find the other 14 hidden objects.

pencil

toothbrush

bird

artist's palette

lemon

turtle

eggplant

banana

teacup

ice-cream cone

jellyfish

mushroom

bean

wedge of orange

candy cane

traffic light

toothbrush

baseball bat

bell

football

butter knife

ring

golf club

sock

comb

horseshoe

sailboat

envelope

fishhook

pennant

drinking straw

needle

light bulb

ax

rubber duck

saltshaker

wristwatch

carrot

artist's brush

toothbrush

wedge of cheese

giraffe

porcupine

salamander

What is the best thing to put into an ice-cream soda?

A straw

pineapple

mushroom

pencil

baseball bat

fish

spoon

arrow

slice of pizza

heart

hammer

bell

butterfly

game piece

pennant

88

Can you hide this ice-cream cone in your own Hidden Pictures drawing?

Buzz over to the hive and find **26** objects in this puzzle!

Knock, knock.
Who's there?
Wayne.
Wayne who?
Wayne does the spelling bee start?

Knock, knock.
Who's there?
Bee.
Bee who?
Because she spelled the word correctly, Nyema won the spelling bee.

Knock, knock.
Who's there?
Spell.
Spell who?
W-H-O.

Make Bubble Wands

YOU NEED:

- scissors
- plastic lid
- hole punch
- tacky craft glue
- wooden craft sticks
- plastic berry basket
- plastic spice-jar insert with holes
- acrylic paints
- clean plastic jar
- ½ cup of liquid dish soap
- ½ cup of water

1. To make a wand, use **scissors** to cut a shape from the **plastic lid** and add holes with a **hole punch**. Using **tacky craft glue**, glue the end of a **wooden craft stick** to the shape as a handle. Let the glue dry.

2. Make other types of wands by cutting a section from a **plastic berry basket**, or use a **plastic spice-jar insert with holes** and glue a wooden craft stick to it. Let the glue dry.

3. To make a jar for your bubble mix, use **acrylic paints** to decorate a **clean plastic jar** with a wide opening and twist-on lid.

4. When the paint is dry, mix the **liquid dish soap** with the **water** in the jar. Then get blowing!

football

drum

spoon

peanut

cupcake

sailboat

juice box

ice-cream cone

bell

glove

comb

rabbit

Can you find these **19** objects hidden in this scene?

fish

paintbrush

teacup

boomerang

slice of pizza

pencil

flashlight

button • heart • ruler • lemon • saucepan • ladle • banana • doughnut • carrot • candle • fish • slice of bread • magnifying glass • hockey stick • sock • crayon • toothbrush • pear

94

Double Cross

To find the answer to the riddle below, first cross out all the pairs of matching letters. Then write the remaining letters in order in the spaces at the bottom of the page. Then find the 4 hidden objects.

LL	BE	CC	PP	CA	FF
US	KK	NN	EH	MM	EW
GG	AS	VV	SS	DD	TH
ET	YY	CC	FF	EA	JJ
RR	CH	HH	KK	EE	ER
AA	SP	TT	ET	BB	PP

Why did the dog get to go on the field trip?

____ ____ ____ ____ ____ ____ ____ ____ ____ ____ ____ ____ ____ ____

____ ____ ____ ____ ____ ____ ____ ____ ____ ____ ____ ____ ____ .

____ ____ ____ ____

Why don't aliens have to clean up after themselves?

Because space is a vacuum

lollipop

horn

teacup

bowling ball

horseshoe

ghost

ring

tack

magnifying glass

crown

pennant

fork

worm

dumbbell

needle

eyeglasses

nail

slice of watermelon

Imagine and Draw

Where did this rocket ship land? Imagine and draw it, then try to find 16 hidden objects.

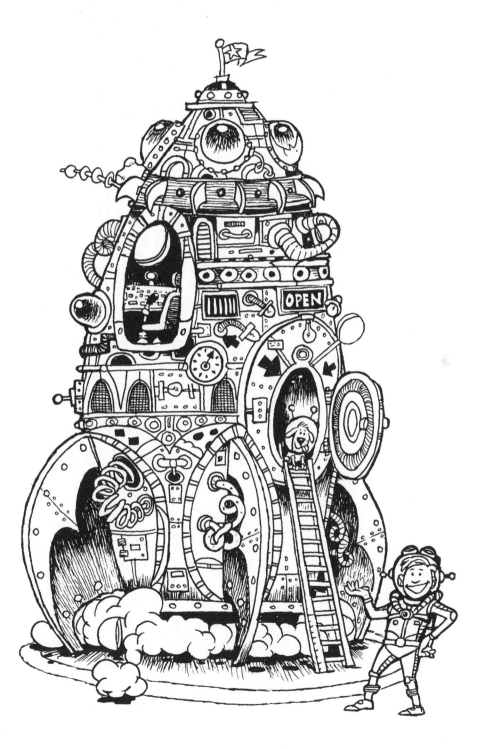

Hidden Word Search

Robbie's shop solves any robot problem.
Can you solve this puzzle and find the 13 hidden objects?

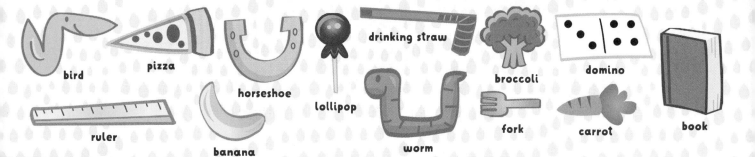

bird
pizza
horseshoe
ruler
banana
lollipop
drinking straw
worm
broccoli
fork
carrot
domino
book

The hidden objects are hidden words, too. Can you find them in the letters below? We found the first one for you.

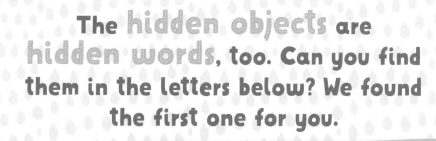

w	h	o	r	s	e	s	h	o	e
a	u	s	r	u	z	u	y	z	h
r	j	d	e	a	n	a	n	a	b
t	i	y	l	h	f	m	t	g	k
s	a	t	u	e	x	y	b	o	w
g	i	h	r	e	d	g	o	e	q
n	l	o	a	r	a	b	k	l	y
i	p	s	i	g	q	v	r	i	h
k	i	b	r	o	c	c	o	l	i
n	z	s	o	q	f	p	f	n	u
i	z	q	f	x	m	d	w	b	y
r	a	i	c	a	r	r	o	t	v
d	l	o	l	l	i	p	o	p	g
h	d	o	n	i	m	o	d	w	z

There's another type of bat in this baseball scene. Find this bat and **18** other objects!

flag

olive

artist's brush

pencil

drumstick

bowl

mug

bird

crescent moon

flashlight

toothbrush

tea bag

duck

tweezers

needle

snake

fish

leaf

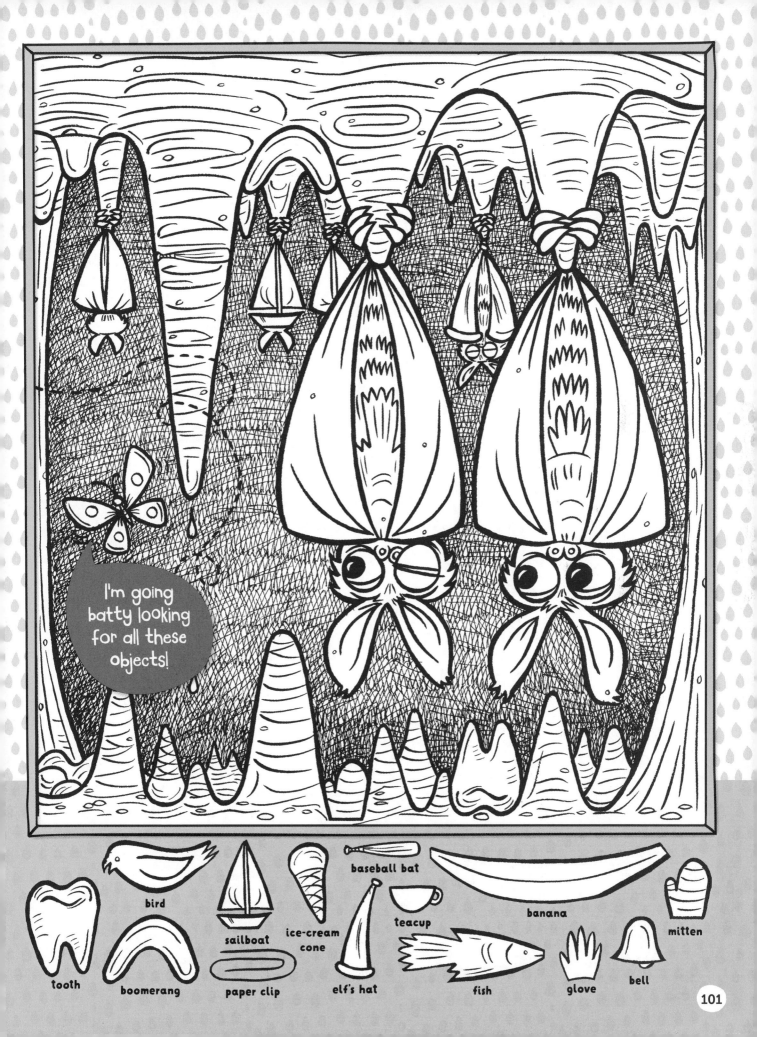

I'm going batty looking for all these objects!

tooth

bird

boomerang

sailboat

paper clip

ice-cream cone

elf's hat

baseball bat

teacup

banana

fish

glove

bell

mitten

We need more singers for our choir! Find **21** birds on the next page.

dart

spoon

doughnut

apple

leaf

apron

baseball cap

mug

boot

safety pin

butter knife

knitted hat

tweezers

golf tee

sailboat

heart

pennant

artist's brush

glove

peach

peanut

fan

lemon

slice of pizza

banana

bell

102

Including these **21**, there have been more than **1,430** birds flying in Hidden Pictures puzzles. There have also been **12** cardinals, **9** doves, **7** crows, **5** woodpeckers, **2** blue jays, and **1** goldfinch.

How do baby birds learn to fly?

They just wing it.

What do birds eat for dessert?

Chocolate-chirp cookies

What do you call two birds in love?

Tweet-hearts

What is a bird's favorite game?

Fly-and-seek

Mixed-Up Hidden Pictures

Unscramble 8 clue names. Then find those hidden objects.

1. tefltrbyu _____

2. hiksohof _____

3. rosohseeh _____

4. sromomuh _____

5. tipbrhuans _____

6. pneepapil _____

7. tohrsotbuh _____

8. eohinbsw _____

Close-Up Hidden Pictures

Slice into this pineapple puzzle. Can you find all 14 hidden objects?

Pineapple leaves can be used to make **cloth**, **ropes**, and **paper**.

The top of the fruit, including the leaves, is called the **crown**.

If you plant the crown of a pineapple in the ground in a warm climate, a new pineapple plant will grow.

Pineapples first grew in **South America**. Today, they grow in warm places all over the world.

The pineapple got its name because it looks like a **pine cone**.

Pineapples take **2** to **3** years to grow.

Pineapples grow from a **plant**, not a tree.

Make Guacamole

Yasir made plenty of guacamole to share with his friends!

YOU NEED:

- 2 avocados
- bowl
- fork
- mild hot sauce
- salt
- ¼ teaspoon dried ginger

1. Have an adult cut the **avocados** in half and take out the pits.

2. Scoop out the flesh of the avocados. Put it in a **bowl** and mash it with a **fork**.

3. Add a few drops of **mild hot sauce**, a few shakes of **salt**, the **dried ginger** to the bowl. Mix it all together.

4. Taste the dip. If you need to, add a bit more of each ingredient until it tastes good.

5. Serve it with chips or other snacks!

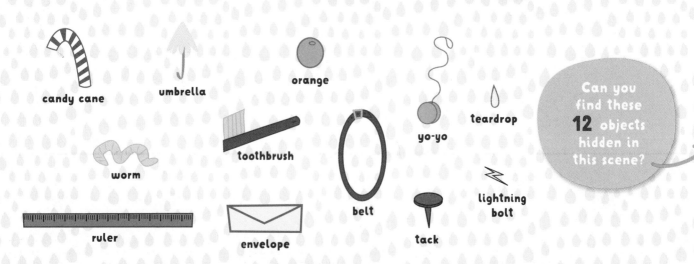

candy cane

umbrella

orange

yo-yo

teardrop

toothbrush

worm

belt

lightning bolt

ruler

envelope

tack

Can you find these **12** objects hidden in this scene?

Find the artist's brush, bridge, comb, envelope, eyeglasses, fire hydrant, magnet, and saw.

This city scene is from the **February 1968** issue of *Highlights*.

This city scene is from the **March 1989** issue of *Highlights*.

Find the baby, boot, briefcase, brush, box, car, comb, drawing board, elephant, fishing pole, flashlight, hat, ice-cream cone, key, mug, radio, ruler, sailboat, shovel, toothbrush, and wallet.

A Silly Fill-In Story

Each teal word in the silly story is also a hidden object. After you read the story, find the objects in the big picture on the next page.

Mateo thought s'mores were the most delicious **SOCK** ever invented. He couldn't wait to make them with his bunkmates. But as the campers gathered around a roaring **BOOMERANG**, Mateo realized that he didn't have a long **GOLF CLUB** to toast the marshmallows. So he started searching the ground for a skinny **LOLLIPOP** to skewer his marshmallows. While looking, he tumbled over a wet **RULER** and broke the chocolate in his **WHALE**.

Just then, a counselor asked, "Who's got the marshmallows?" *Uh-oh!* Mateo raised his **HEART**. He had goofed again. That afternoon, Mateo had stretched out on the **SLICE OF BREAD** near the **ROCKET SHIP** court. The hot **OAR** had made him sleepy. He had rested his **CANDY CORN** on the plastic bag. Before long, Mateo had fallen asleep. When he woke up, he realized he had squished the entire **ADHESIVE BANDAGE** of marshmallows. They were totally flat.

Mateo opened his **ARROW** and pulled out the bag. He said, "I squished them. Sorry, guys." The campers' groans soon turned to cheers: The flat marshmallows fit perfectly on a flat graham **FOOTBALL**.

"Best s'mores ever!" declared Mateo's buddy Nick.

There it is, Zurkle. The machine they use to punish humans who misbehave!

It's horrifying, Zatz! They strap them in and make them go up and down, around and around really fast.

Zatz and Zurkle

Here's what Zatz and Zurkle called the objects they found. Can you find them, too?

snugtoe

pinchy

sritchit

warmzie

tastilick

comeback

squirmo

holdit

stitchy

owzie

moveme

zipzip

cutcut

boingboing

When they are done screaming, I suppose they have learned their lesson.

Yes, but why do some of them stand in line to get punished AGAIN?

Find the dragonfly, fish, fishhook, flowers in a vase, hammer, ice-cream cone, ladybug, lamp, mouse, pencil, snail, sock, telephone receiver, and turtle.

This puzzle was in the **first annual** Hidden Pictures annual collection in **1998**.

Hidden Pictures
1 9 9 8
More Than 450 Hidden Objects

With Picture and Word Clues

What type of phone does your family use today?

game controller   lollipop   ring   fork   telescope   slice of pizza   sock   shoe   flashlight   musical note   ice-cream cone   guitar   elf's hat   apple   basketball   toothbrush

6 by Six

Each of these small scenes contains 6 hidden objects from the list below. Some objects are hidden in more than one scene. Can you find the 6 hidden objects in each scene?

artist's brush (3)	paper clip (4)
baseball bat (3)	ring (2)
bell (4)	shoe (2)
domino (3)	spoon (2)
ice-cream cone (2)	tack (5)
lollipop (3)	toothbrush (3)

The numbers tell you how many times each object is hidden.

116

BONUS MATCH

Two scenes contain the exact same set of hidden objects. Can you find that matching pair?

closed umbrella

trowel

drumstick

key

crayon

game piece

hamburger

cinnamon bun

slice of watermelon

boomerang

sock

tomato

wedge of lemon

118

... or up in the sky?

snake

crayon

toothbrush

wedge of lemon

fish

snow cone

teacup

ice-cream cone

domino

snowman

pencil

adhesive bandage

ball of yarn

slice of pizza

Take Two

Each of these scenes contains **12** hidden objects, which are listed on the next page. But each object is only **hidden once**. Which object is in which scene?

banana	drum	game piece	oven mitt	slice of pizza
bell	drumstick	ice-cream cone	peanut	snake
bird	envelope	ice-cream bar	sailboat	tooth
boomerang	fishhook	lollipop	screwdriver	toothbrush
candy cane	fried egg	magnet	skateboard	

Do you prefer to watch the Winter Olympics or the Summer Olympics?

ruler

feather

flag

mitten

wishbone

ring

spatula

mug

eyeglasses

slice of pizza

fishhook

heart

toothbrush

Which animals would be good at which sports? Why?

fishhook domino boomerang broccoli comb toothbrush fish banana snake saucepan book

umbrella slice of cake musical note party hat pencil canoe cupcake

Just Sayin' . . .

Give this bird something to think. Then find the hidden
BANANA, BROOM, CARROT, CRESCENT MOON, and **PENCIL.**

This micrograph of a wood cell is hiding **23** bowling pins. Can you find them all?

Start

Finish

Find this wedge of cheese

along with **7** other objects. Then help the baby turtle find a path to the water.

bus

pencil

crescent moon

chick

ear of corn

elbow noodle

lemon

What music should you avoid at a hot-air balloon festival?

pop

teapot

toothbrush

fish

saw

apple

flowerpot

peanut

banana

handbag

ladder

drum

carrot

belt

feather

scissors

rolling pin

crown

mushroom

tube of toothpaste

ladle

slice of pizza

key

flashlight

ANSWERS

Page 3

Pages 4–5

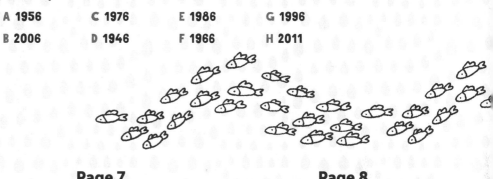

Mixed-Up Covers

A 1956	C 1976	E 1986	G 1996
B 2006	D 1946	F 1966	H 2011

Page 6

Page 7

Page 8

Page 9

Page 10

Page 14

ANSWERS

Page 15

Page 16

Page 17

Page 18

Page 19

Page 20

Page 21

Page 22

Page 23

ANSWERS

Page 24

Page 26

Page 27

Page 28

Page 29

Page 30

Page 31

Page 32

ANSWERS

Page 33

Pages 34—35

Page 36

Page 37

Page 38

Page 39

Page 40

Page 41

NONE. THEY HAVE BEAR FEET.

ANSWERS

Pages 42–43

1. snowman	11. saltshaker	20. funnel
2. party hat	12. ring	21. belt
3. artist's brush	13. muffin	22. fork
4. baseball cap	14. mushroom	23. spoon
5. gold club	15. glove	24. teacup
6. heart	16. pencil	25. baseball
7. fish	17. ladle	26. crescent moon
8. scissors	18. wedge of lemon	27. sock
9. jump rope	19. screwdriver	28. fishhook
10. mop		29. slice of pizza

Page 44

Page 46

Page 48

Page 49

Page 50

Page 51

ANSWERS

Pages 52–53

Page 55

Page 56

Page 57

Page 58

Page 59

Pages 60–61

ANSWERS

These puzzles make my tail wag!

Page 62

Page 63

Pages 64–65

```
h  w  t  x  m  i  v  d  a  s
s  e  a  s  h  e  l  l  r  u
h  d  o  m  i  n  o  e  g  i
o  g  b  d  c  t  r  t  n  t
r  e  l  i  a  o  q  a  a  c
s  o  f  a  n  x  e  h  h  a
e  l  a  u  e  v  a  y  t  s
s  i  s  n  i  m  a  a  o  c
h  m  r  h  y  z  p  t  a  f
o  e  e  s  z  h  s  r  c  b
b  v  p  f  i  y  j  a  g  n
e  n  v  c  j  f  p  m  g  e
r  h  a  i  r  d  r  y  e  r
```

Page 66

Page 67

Pages 68–69

137

ANSWERS

Pages 70–71

Page 72

Page 73

Page 74

Page 75

Pages 76–77

Page 78

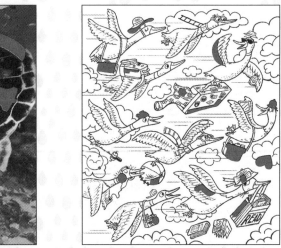

ANSWERS

Page 79

Page 80

Page 81

Page 82

Pages 84–85

Page 86

Page 87

Page 88

ANSWERS

Page 90

Page 91

Pages 92–93

Page 94

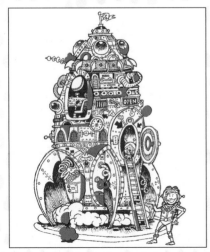

Page 95

BECAUSE HE WAS THE
TEACHER'S PET

Page 96

Page 97

Pages 98–99

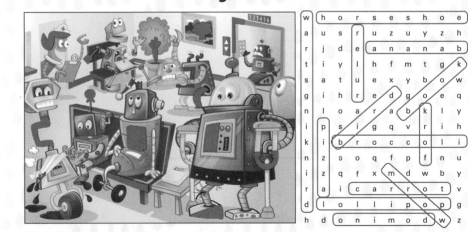

ANSWERS

Page 100

Page 101

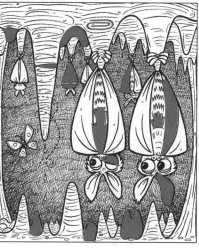

Page 102

Page 103

Page 104

Page 105

Pages 106—107

Page 108

Page 109

ANSWERS

Page 111

Page 112–113

Page 114

Page 115

Pages 116–117

Page 118

142

ANSWERS

Page 119

Pages 120–121

Page 122

Page 123

Page 124

Page 125

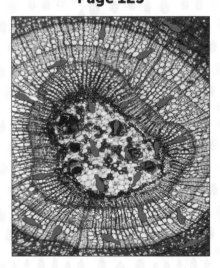

Page 126

Page 127

ANSWERS

Pages 128–129

Page 130

Contributing Illustrators: Lynn Adams (page 36); Lois Axeman (56); Paula J. Becker (42–43, 126); Iryna Bodnaruk (23, 68–69, 87); Karen Stormer Brooks (122); Alice Chapin (3); Dave Clegg (95); Josh Cleland (11, 94); Laura Ferraro Close (80); Olivia Cole (50); Daryll Collins (37); Mark Corcoran (81); David Coulson (124); Jef Czekaj (120–121); Mike Dammer (98–99); Tim Davis (8, 20, 21, 66, 101); Mike DeSantis (40); Chuck Dillon (79, 85); Luke Flowers (72, 115); Rocky Fuller (88); Mernie Gallagher-Cole (62); John Gee (74); Patrick Girouard (118); Bill Golliher (46–47, 125); Valeri Gorbachev (114); Barry Gott (91); Peter Grosshauser (111); Susan T. Hall (119); Jennifer Harney (6, 27, 73, 127); Marilee Harrald-Pilz (96); David Helton (32, 49, 105); Jannie Ho (15); Deborah Johnson (100); Charles Jordan (57); Gideon Kendall (34–35, 112–113); Kelly Kennedy (18, 28–29, 93); Dave Klug (9, 44, 104); Ken Krug (76–77); Gary LaCoste (19, 86); Newton LeVine (108); Pat Lewis (24, 58, 123); Ron Lieser (10); James Loram (22); Lyn Martin (59); Susan Miller (48); Gary Mohrman (97); Julissa Mora (16); Mike Moran (25, 45, 64–65, 89, 107); Mitch Mortimer (31, 78); Neil Numberman (4–5, 52–53, 116–117, 130), R. Michael Palan (67); Tamara Petrosino (14, 30, 60–61); Rich Powell (51); Hazel Quintanilla (39); Kevin Rechin (26, 70–71, 103); Dana Regan (17); Christine Schneider (128–129); Joe Seidita (90); Jeri Simkus (109); Jamie Smith (7); Mary Sullivan (55); Maggie Swanson (75); Linda Weller (63); Brian White (33, 38, 41); Kevin Zimmer (4); Diana Zourelias (82, 102)

Photos by beholdingeye/iStock (125); damedeeso/Getty (46–47); vlad61/Getty (76–77)

Cover art by Mike Lowery

Published by Highlights Press
815 Church Street
Honesdale, Pennsylvania 18431
ISBN: 978-1-64472-508-5
Manufactured in Mattoon, IL, USA
Mfg. 05/2021
First edition
Visit our website at Highlights.com.
10 9 8 7 6 5 4 3 2 1